Life Cycle of a Guinea Pig

Angela Royston

Heinemann
LIBRARY

First published in Great Britain by Heinemann Library
Halley Court, Jordan Hill, Oxford OX2 8EJ
a division of Reed Educational and Professional Publishing Ltd

Heinemann is a registered trademark of Reed Educational and Professional
Publishing Limited.

Oxford   Florence   Prague   Madrid   Athens   Melbourne
Auckland   Kuala Lumpur   Singapore   Tokyo   Ibadan
Nairobi   Kampala   Johannesburg   Gaborone   Portsmouth NH
Chicago   Mexico City   São Paulo

Designed by Celia Floyd
Illustrations by Alan Fraser
Printed In Hong Kong by South China Printing Co. (1988) Ltd

02 01 00 99 98
10 9 8 7 6 5 4 3 2 1

ISBN 0 431 08365 7

British Library Cataloguing in Publication Data

Royston, Angela
  Life cycle of a guinea pig
  1.Guinea pigs - Juvenile literature
  I.Title II.Guinea pig
  599.3'592

Acknowledgements
The Publisher would like to thank the following for permission to reproduce
photographs:
Bruce Coleman Ltd/Dr Eckart Potts p4; Lanceau/Cogis pp5, 25; Leibenswerte
Neerschweinchen, Elrig Hansen c 1998 Kinder Buchverlag Luzern (Sauerlander AG)
pp6–9, 11–13, 16, 17, 19–22; NHPA/Daniel Heuclin p24; NHPA/Jany Sauvanet p26;
NHPA/Kevin Schafer p14; OSF/W Layer p18; South American Pictures/Tony
Morrison p27 Testu/Cogis p15; Vidal/Cogis p23.

Cover photograph: Lanceau/Cogis

Contents

Meet the guinea pigs

A guinea pig is a small, furry animal with large front teeth. Guinea pigs belong to a group of animals called cavies.

Newborn

I day

I week

Capybara

The capybara is the largest kind of cavy. Wild guinea pigs are brown. The guinea pigs in this book are brown, white and black.

1 month

8 months

10 months

Newborn

This female guinea pig is ready to give birth. First one tiny **pup** slides out. It is soon followed by another, and another.

Newborn

I day

I week

The pups are wet and sticky, so the mother licks them clean. The pups open their eyes and look around.

1 month

8 months

10 months

First day

This **pup** is still wet. She can see and hear, and is soon running about. She sniffs the hay and starts to explore.

Newborn

I day

I week

She has smelt milk! She pushes her head under her mother and finds a **teat**. Now she is having her first drink of milk.

1 month

8 months

10 months

1 week

The **pups** are very timid and keep close to their mother. This one is nibbling some grass with her long front teeth.

Newborn

1 day

1 week

A loud noise scares the pups. They hide in the long grass until one of them pokes his head out to see if it's safe.

1 month

8 months

10 months

1 month

The little guinea pigs love to play.
They sniff, rush around and squeak
loudly. This **pup** is doing a
handstand!

Newborn

1 day

1 week

When they are tired, they snuggle up together for a short nap. They know their mother's smell and they know each other's.

1 month

8 months

10 months

2–5 months

Wild guinea pigs are always on the lookout for danger. When this huge **condor** flies overhead, the little guinea pigs are terrified.

Newborn

1 day

1 week

Guinea pigs cannot run very fast on their short legs. This guinea pig stands completely still instead, so the condor does not notice him.

8 months

The guinea pigs are fully grown now and ready to have a family of their own. A large brown male joins the group.

Newborn

I day

I week

He growls deeply and creeps around one of the female guinea pigs. The female sniffs his face and soon they **mate**.

1 month

8 months

10 months

63 days later

For 63 days baby guinea pigs grow inside the female. She gets very hungry and eats more food. She loves this juicy sweetcorn!

Newborn

1 day

1 week

Then one day she hides away in the grass, and her babies are born. She pulls away the sticky bag that covers each one.

1 month

8 months

10 months

1–3 weeks

The new mother works hard looking after her **pups**. She licks them to keep them clean and they soon know her smell.

Newborn

1 day

1 week

She watches over the pups as they play in the straw. When she gives a special grunt, they rush to her to drink her milk.

1 month

8 months

10 months

3 weeks

The young **pups** keep close to their mother. When she walks away, they scurry after her.

Newborn

I day

I week

The pups grow quickly and are soon able to join all the other guinea pigs. Many new pups have been born and are growing up.

I month

8 months

10 months

1–8 years

Wild guinea pigs have many enemies. **Pumas** and other animals eat guinea pigs. Snakes, like this boa, would like to snatch one for a meal.

Newborn

I day

I week

This guinea pig is sniffing the air. He smells a snake coming and hides in the grass. Not all the guinea pigs are so lucky.

1 month

8 months

10 months

Living with people

Wild guinea pigs come from
South America. They live on
the grassy **plains** and on the
slopes of the Andes mountains.

These guinea pigs are kept by people who live in the Andes mountains. Guinea pigs kept as pets may live for up to 8 years.

Life cycle

Newborn pup

1 week old

1 month old

8 months old

10 months old

Fact file

A guinea pig's front teeth never stop growing. Pet guinea pigs need to chew carrots or even a piece of wood to stop their teeth becoming too long.

A guinea pig is about 30 centimetres long – as long as a ruler – and weighs about 0.5 kilogrammes.

A female may have up to four **pups** at the same time, but she has only two **teats**, so the pups have to take turns to feed.

Glossary

condor   a large bird that lives in the Andes mountains of South America

mate   to come together (a female and a male) to produce young

plains   flat, open countryside

puma   a large, wild cat that lives in the Andes mountains of South America

pup   a young guinea pig from the time it is born until it is old enough to look after itself

teat   a place from where a baby can drink milk from its mother

Index